THE WEDDING MASS
READINGS, PRAYERS AND BLESSINGS

THE
WEDDING
MASS

Readings, Prayers and Blessings

VERITAS

Published 2011 by
Veritas Publications
7–8 Lower Abbey Street
Dublin 1, Ireland
Email publications@veritas.ie
Website www.veritas.ie

ISBN 978 1 84730 319 6
Copyright © Veritas, 2011

10 9 8 7 6

A catalogue record for this book is available from the British
Library.

Scripture Readings are taken from *The Jerusalem Bible*, © 1966 by
Darton, Longman & Todd, Ltd. Psalms are taken from *The Psalms: A
New Translation*, © 1963, The Grail (England).

Cover design by Barbara Croatto, Veritas
Printed in the Republic of Ireland by Anglo Printers Ltd, Drogheda

*Veritas books are printed on paper made from the wood pulp of managed
forests. For every tree felled, at least one tree is planted, thereby renewing
natural resources.*

Preface

This booklet seeks to help you in choosing the readings for the occasion of your Wedding Mass. It also includes a selection of intentions for the Prayer of the Faithful that you might wish to adapt or use as inspiration when composing your own, as well as blessings and reflections that celebrate marriage.

Contents

Introduction to Choosing Readings

Adapted from *A Wedding of Your Own* by Padraig McCarthy (Veritas, 2003), *Readings for Your Wedding* by Brian Magee CM (Veritas, 1995) and *To Love and to Cherish* by Oliver Brennan (Veritas, 2006).

For the Wedding Mass, the first reading is taken from the Old Testament. It is then followed by the responsorial psalm. Normally the responsorial psalm will be sung, but if it is to be read, remember that it is a poem and has a musical rhythm. An introduction is supplied here for each psalm to help the couple to choose a particular psalm. The cantor or reader should help the congregation to remember the psalm response by repeating it with them the first time, but should never cue them in by saying 'Response!' The second reading is taken from the New Testament. The Gospel Acclamation is sung or said before the Gospel Reading is proclaimed by the priest.

The Gospel passages are included so that you as a couple and the priest may choose an appropriate one, and perhaps talk about what will be said in the homily. All the readings are taken from *The Jerusalem Bible*. The Prayer of the Faithful follows the celebration of the Rite of Marriage. Those included here can be used as they appear, but also serve as inspiration and direction when composing your own personal prayers.

Choosing the readings for your wedding is an important task. These texts will speak to you of the meaning of your love and marriage. Maybe there's a reading you've heard so often at weddings that you wouldn't feel properly married without it! The texts will be familiar enough, but new light will always be thrown on them by the circumstances in which they are heard.

The Wedding Mass readings have been chosen not only because they have something human and beautiful to say about love and marriage, but mainly because they express the Christian understanding of marriage. A Christian wedding is a celebration of the Sacrament of Matrimony, where words and actions come together to express the deepest meanings of marriage.

First Reading

Old Testament Readings

✸ Reading 1
A reading from the book of Genesis 1:26-28. 31

Male and female he created them.

God said, 'Let us make men in our own image, in the likeness of ourselves, and let them be masters of the fish of the sea, the birds of heaven, the cattle, all the wild beasts and all the reptiles that crawl upon the earth.'

> God created man in the image of himself,
> in the image of God he created him,
> male and female he created them.

God blessed them, saying to them, 'Be fruitful, multiply, fill the earth and conquer it. Be masters of the fish of the sea, the birds of heaven and all the living animals on the earth.' God saw all he had made, and indeed it was very good.

The word of the Lord.

✤ ✸ Reading 2

A reading from the book of Genesis 2:18-24

They become one body.

The Lord God said, 'It is not good that the man should be alone. I will make him a helpmate.' So from the soil the Lord God fashioned all the wild beasts and all the birds of heaven. These he brought to the man to see what he would call them; each one was to bear the name the man would give it. The man gave names to all the cattle, all the birds of heaven and all the wild beasts. But no helpmate suitable for man was found for him. So the Lord God made the man fall into a deep sleep. And while he slept, he took one of his ribs and enclosed it in flesh. The Lord God built the rib he had taken from the man into a woman, and brought her to the man. The man said:

'This at last is bone from my bones,
and flesh from my flesh!
This is to be called woman,
for this was taken from man.'

This is why a man leaves his father and mother and joins himself to his wife, and they become one body.

The word of the Lord.

❁ Reading 3

A reading from the book of Proverbs 31:10-13. 19-20. 30-31

The woman who fears the Lord is the one to praise.

A perfect wife – who can find her?
She is far beyond the price of pearls.
Her husband's heart has confidence in her,
from her he will derive no little profit.
Advantage and not hurt she brings him
all the days of her life.
She is always busy with wool and with flax,
she does her work with eager hands.
She sets her hands to the distaff,
her fingers grasp the spindle.
She holds out her hand to the poor,
she opens her arms to the needy.
Charm is deceitful, and beauty empty;
the woman who is wise is the one to praise.
Give her a share in what her hands have worked for,
and let her works tell her praises at the city gates.

The word of the Lord.

✸ Reading 4

A reading from the book of Genesis 24:48-51. 58-67

Isaac loved Rebekah, and so he was consoled for the loss of his mother.

Abraham's servant said to Laban, 'I blessed the Lord, God of my master Abraham, who had graciously led me to choose the daughter of my master's brother for his son. Now tell me whether you are prepared to show kindness and goodness to my master; if not, say so, and I shall know what to do.'

Laban and Bethuel replied, 'This is from the Lord; it is not in our power to say yes or no to you. Rebekah is there before you. Take her and go; and let her become the wife of your master's son, as the Lord has decreed.' They called Rebekah and asked her, 'Do you want to leave with this man?' 'I do,' she replied. Accordingly they let their sister Rebekah go, with her nurse, and Abraham's servant and his men. They blessed Rebekah in these words:

'Sister of ours, increase
    to thousands and tens of thousands!
May your descendants gain possession
    of the gates of their enemies!'

Rebekah and her servants stood up, mounted the camels, and followed the man. The servant took Rebekah and departed.

Isaac, who lived in the Negeb, had meanwhile come into the wilderness of the well of Lahai Roi. Now Isaac went walking in the fields as evening fell, and looking up saw camels approaching. And Rebekah looked up and saw Isaac. She jumped down from her camel, and asked the servant, 'Who is that man walking through the fields to meet us?' The servant replied, 'That is my master.' Then she took her veil and covered herself up. The servant told Isaac the whole story; and Isaac led Rebekah into his tent and made her his wife; and he loved her. And so Isaac was consoled for the loss of his mother.

The word of the Lord.

✹ Reading 5

A reading from the book of Tobit 7:6-14

The Lord of heaven favour you, my child, and grant you his grace and peace.

Raguel kissed Tobias and wept. Then finding words, he said, 'Blessings on you, child! You are the son of a noble father. How sad it is that someone so virtuous and full of good deeds should have gone blind!' He fell on the neck of his kinsman Tobias and wept. And his wife Edna wept for him, and so did his daughter Sarah. Raguel killed a sheep from the flock, and they gave Tobias and Raphael a warm-hearted welcome.

They washed and bathed and sat down to table. Then Tobias said to Raphael, 'Brother Azarias, will you ask Raguel to give me my sister Sarah?' Raguel overheard the words, and said to the young man, 'Eat and drink, and make the most of your evening; no one else has the right to take my daughter Sarah – no one but you, my brother. In any case I, for my own part, am not at liberty to give her to anyone else, since you are her next of kin. However, my boy, I must be frank with you: I have tried to find a husband for her seven times among our kinsmen, and all of them have died the first evening, on going to her room. But for the present, my boy, eat and drink; the Lord will grant you his grace and peace.' Tobias spoke out, 'I will not hear of eating and drinking till you have come to a decision about me.' Raguel answered, 'Very well. Since, as prescribed by the Book of Moses, she is given to you, heaven itself decrees she shall be yours. I shall therefore entrust your sister to you. From now you are her brother and she is your sister. She is given to you from today for ever. The Lord of heaven favour you tonight, my child, and grant you his grace and peace.' Raguel called for his daughter Sarah, took her by the hand and gave her to Tobias with these words, 'I entrust her to you; the law and the ruling recorded in the Book of Moses assign her to you as your wife. Take her; take her home to your father's house with a good conscience. The God of heaven grant you a good journey in peace.' Then he turned to her mother and asked her to fetch him writing paper. He drew up the marriage contract, how he gave his daughter as bride to Tobias according to the ordinance in the Law of Moses.

After this they began to eat and drink.

The word of the Lord.

✸ Reading 6
A reading from the book of Tobit 8:4-8

Bring us to old age together.

On the evening of their marriage, Tobias said to Sarah, 'You and I must pray and petition our Lord to win his grace and protection.' They began praying for protection, and this was how he began:

'You are blessed, O God of our fathers;
blessed, too, is your name
for ever and ever.
Let the heavens bless you
and all things you have made
for evermore.
It was you who created Adam,
you who created Eve his wife
to be his help and support;
and from these two the human race was born.
It was you who said,
"It is not right that the man should be alone;
let us make him a helpmate like himself."
And so I do not take my sister
for any lustful motive;
I do it in singleness of heart.
Be kind enough to have pity on her and on me
and bring us to old age together.'

And together they said, 'Amen, Amen'.

The word of the Lord.

✸ Reading 7
A reading from the Song of Songs 2:8-10. 14. 16; 8:6-7

Love is strong as Death.

I hear my Beloved.
See how he comes
leaping on the mountains,
bounding over the hills.
My Beloved is like a gazelle,
like a young stag.
See where he stands
behind our wall.
He looks in at the window,
he peers through the lattice.
My Beloved lifts up his voice,
he says to me,
'Come then, my love,
my lovely one, come.
My dove, hiding in the clefts of the rock.
In the coverts of the cliff,
show me your face,
let me hear your voice;
for your voice is sweet
and your face is beautiful.'

My beloved is mine and I am his.
Set me like a seal on your heart,
like a seal on your arm.
For love is strong as Death,
passion as relentless as Sheol.
The flash of it is a flash of fire,
a flame of the Lord himself.
Love no floods can quench,
no torrents drown.

The word of the Lord.

✺ Reading 8

✝ A reading from the book of Ecclesiasticus 26:1-4. 13-16

Like the sun rising is the beauty of a good wife in a well-kept house.

Happy the husband of a really good wife;
the number of his days will be doubled.
A perfect wife is the joy of her husband,
he will live out the years of his life in peace.
A good wife is the best of portions,
reserved for those who fear the Lord;
rich or poor, they will be glad of heart;
cheerful of face, whatever the season.
The grace of a wife will charm her husband,
her accomplishments will make him stronger.
A silent wife is a gift from the Lord,
no price can be put on a well-trained character.
A modest wife is a boon twice over,
a chaste character cannot be weighed on scales.
Like the sun rising over the mountains of the Lord
is the beauty of a good wife in a well-kept house.

The word of the Lord.

❀ Reading 9
A reading from the prophet Jeremiah 31:31-34

I will make a new covenant with the House of Israel and the House of Judah.

See, the days are coming – it is the Lord who speaks, when I will make a new covenant with the House of Israel and the House of Judah, but not a covenant like the one I made with their ancestors on the day I took them by the hand to bring them out of the land of Egypt. No, this is the covenant I shall make with the House of Israel when those days arrive – it is the Lord who speaks. Deep within them I will plant my Law, writing it on their hearts. Then I will be their God and they shall be my people. There will be no further need for neighbour to try to teach neighbour, or brother to say to brother, 'Learn to know the Lord!' No, they will all know me, the least no less than the greatest – it is the Lord who speaks.

The word of the Lord.

✹ Reading 10

(It is appropriate to use this reading as the First Reading in the Easter Season.)

A reading from the book of the Apocalypse 19:1. 5-9

Happy are those who are invited to the wedding feast of the Lamb.

I, John, seemed to hear the great sound of a huge crowd in heaven, singing, 'Alleluia! Victory and glory and power to our God!'

Then a voice came from the throne; it said, 'Praise our God, you servants of his and all who, great or small, revere him.' And I heard what seemed to be the voices of a huge crowd, like the sound of the ocean or the great roar of thunder, answering, 'Alleluia! The reign of the Lord our God Almighty has begun; let us be glad and joyful and give glory to God, because this is the time for the marriage of the Lamb. His bride is ready, and she has been able to dress herself in dazzling white linen, because her linen is made of the good deeds of the saints.' The angel said, 'Write this, "Happy are those who are invited to the wedding feast of the Lamb."'

The word of the Lord.

Responsorial Psalm

❀ **Responsorial Psalm 1**

Ps 32:12. 18. 20-22. R v.5

God's love and care are seen in all the works of creation, and in human love.We can indeed respond to the Psalm saying:

R. The Lord fills the earth with his love.

1. They are happy, whose God is the Lord,
   the people he has chosen as his own.
   The Lord looks on those who revere him,
   on those who hope in his love. (R)

2. Our soul is waiting for the Lord.
   The Lord is our help and our shield.
   In him do our hearts find joy.
   We trust in his holy name. (R)

3. May your love be upon us, O Lord,
   as we place all our hope in you. (R)

❧ Responsorial Psalm 2

Ps 148:1-4. 9-14. R v.12

When we look at the marvellous ways of God in his creation we are led to respond:

R. Praise the name of the Lord.

or

R. Alleluia!

1. Praise the Lord from the heavens,
   praise him in the heights.
   Praise him, all his angels,
   praise him, all his host. (R)

2. Praise him, sun and moon,
   praise him, shining stars.
   Praise him, highest heavens
   and the waters above the heavens. (R)

3. All mountains and hills,
   all fruit trees and cedars,
   beasts, wild and tame,
   reptiles and birds on the wing. (R)

4. All earth's kings and peoples,
   earth's princes and rulers:
   young men and maidens,
   old men together with children. (R)

5. Let them praise the name of the Lord
   for he alone is exalted.
   The splendour of his name
   reaches beyond heaven and earth. (R)

❧ Responsorial Psalm 3
Ps 144:8-10. 15. 17-18. R v.9

The power of God is seen in the marriage of Isaac and Rebekah. He protects all who trust in him; in our response to the psalm we thank him for that care:

R. How good is the Lord to all.

1. The Lord is kind and full of compassion,
   slow to anger, abounding in love.
   How good is the Lord to all,
   compassionate to all his creatures. (R)

2. All your creatures shall thank you, O Lord,
   and your friends shall repeat their blessing.
   The eyes of all creatures look to you
   and you give them their food in due time. (R)

3. The Lord is just in all his ways
   and loving in all his deeds.
   He is close to all who call him,
   who call on him from their hearts. (R)

❧ Responsorial Psalm 4

Ps 32:12. 18. 20-22. R v.5

R. The Lord fills the earth with his love.

1. They are happy, whose God is the Lord,
   the people he has chosen as his own.
   The Lord looks on those who revere him,
   on those who hope in his love. (R)

2. Our soul is waiting for the Lord.
   The Lord is our help and our shield.
   In him do our hearts find joy.
   We trust in his holy name. (R)

3. May your love be upon us, O Lord,
   as we place all our hope in you. (R)

◈ **Responsorial Psalm 5**

Ps 102:1-2. 8. 13. 17-18. R v.8. Alt. R v.17

Respect for the laws of God is our response to the love that he shows us first; we acknowledge his love in our response:

R. The Lord is compassion and love.

or

R. The love of the Lord is everlasting upon those who hold him in fear.

1. My soul, give thanks to the Lord,
   all my being, bless his holy name.
   My soul, give thanks to the Lord
   and never forget all his blessings. (R)

2. The Lord is compassion and love,
   slow to anger and rich in mercy.
   As a father has compassion on his sons,
   the Lord has pity on those who fear him. (R)

3. The love of the Lord is everlasting
   upon those who hold him in fear;
   his justice reaches out to children's children
   when they keep his covenant in truth. (R)

✻ Responsorial Psalm 6

Ps 127:1-5. R cf. v.1. Alt. R v.4

The blessings of a united family life are praised in this psalm; our response thanks God for such happiness:

R. O blessed are those who fear the Lord!

or

R. Indeed thus shall be blessed the man who fears the Lord.

1. O blessed are those who fear the Lord
   and walk in his ways!
   By the labour of your hands you shall eat.
   You will be happy and prosper. (R)

2. Your wife will be like a fruitful vine
   in the heart of your house;
   your children like shoots of the olive,
   around your table. (R)

3. Indeed thus shall be blessed
   the man who fears the Lord.
   May the Lord bless you from Zion
   all the days of your life. (R)

❧ Responsorial Psalm 7

Ps 33:2-9. R v.2. Alt. R v.9

R. I will bless the Lord at all times.

or

R. Taste and see that the Lord is good.

1. I will bless the Lord at all times,
   his praise always on my lips;
   in the Lord my soul shall make its boast.
   The humble shall hear and be glad. (R)

2. Glorify the Lord with me.
   Together let us praise his name.
   I sought the Lord and he answered me;
   from all my terrors he set me free. (R)

3. Look towards him and be radiant;
   let your faces not be abashed.
   This poor man called; the Lord heard him
   and rescued him from all his distress. (R)

4. The angel of the Lord is encamped
   around those who revere him, to rescue them.
   Taste and see that the Lord is good.
   He is happy who seeks refuge in him. (R)

❀ Responsorial Psalm 8
Ps 111:1-9. R cf. v.1

Peace and contentment come to those who live with a good conscience, who live according to the will of God. The message of this psalm is summed up in our response:

R. Happy the man who takes delight in the Lord's commands.
or
R. Alleluia!

1. Happy the man who fears the Lord,
   who takes delight in his commands.
   His sons will be powerful on earth;
   the children of the upright are blessed. (R)

2. Riches and wealth are in his house;
   his justice stands firm for ever.
   He is a light in the darkness for the upright:
   he is generous, merciful and just. (R)

3. The good man takes pity and lends,
   he conducts his affairs with honour.
   The just man will never waver:
   he will be remembered for ever. (R)

4. He has no fears of evil news;
   with a firm heart he trusts in the Lord.
   With a steadfast heart he will not fear;
   he will see the downfall of his foes. (R)

5. Open-handed, he gives to the poor;
   his justice stands firm forever.
   His head will be raised in glory. (R)

✄ ❧ Responsorial Psalm 9

Ps 148:1-4. 9-12. R v.12

The response 'Alleluia' is very appropriate during the Easter season. It means Praise the Lord: we join in the praise with our response:

R. Praise the name of the Lord.

or

R. Alleluia!

1. Praise the Lord from the heavens,
   praise him in the heights.
   Praise him, all his angels,
   praise him, all his host. (R)

2. Praise him, sun and moon,
   praise him, shining stars.
   Praise him, highest heavens
   and the waters above the heavens. (R)

3. All mountains and hills,
   all fruit trees and cedars,
   beasts, wild and tame,
   reptiles and birds on the wing. (R)

4. All earth's kings and peoples,
   earth's princes and rulers:
   young men and maidens,
   old men together with children. (R)

5. Let them praise the name of the Lord,
   for he alone is exalted.
   The splendour of his name
   reaches beyond heaven and earth. (R)

Second Reading

New Testament Readings

✳ Reading 1

A reading from the letter of St Paul to the Romans 8:31-35. 37-39

Nothing can come between us and the love of Christ.

With God on our side who can be against us? Since God did not spare his own Son but gave him up to benefit us all, we may be certain, after such a gift, that he will not refuse anything he can give. Could anyone accuse those that God has chosen? When God acquits, could anyone condemn? Could Christ Jesus? No! He not only died for us – he rose from the dead and there at God's right hand he stands and pleads for us.

Nothing therefore can come between us and the love of Christ, even if we are troubled or worried or being persecuted, or lacking food or clothes, or being threatened or even attacked. These are the trials through which we triumph, by the power of him who loved us.

For I am certain of this: neither death nor life, no angel, no prince, nothing that exists, nothing still to come, not any power, or height or depth, nor any created thing, can ever come between us and the love of God made visible in Christ Jesus our Lord.

The word of the Lord.

✖ Reading 2
A reading from the letter of St Paul to the Romans 12:1-2. 9-18

Offering your living bodies as a holy sacrifice, truly pleasing to him.

Think of God's mercy, my brothers, and worship him, I beg you, in a way that is worthy of thinking beings, by offering your living bodies as a holy sacrifice, truly pleasing to God. Do not model yourselves on the behaviour of the world around you, but let your behaviour change, modelled by your new mind. This is the only way to discover the will of God and know what is good, what it is that God wants, what is the perfect thing to do.

Do not let your love be a pretence, but sincerely prefer good to evil. Love each other as much as brothers should, and have a profound respect for each other. Work for the Lord with untiring effort and with great earnestness of spirit. If you have hope, this will make you cheerful. Do not give up if trials come; and keep on praying. If any of the saints are in need you must share with them; and you should make hospitality your special care.

Bless those who persecute you: never curse them, bless them. Rejoice with those who rejoice and be sad with those in sorrow. Treat everyone with equal kindness; never be condescending but make real friends with the poor. Do not allow yourself to become self-satisfied. Never repay evil with evil but let everyone see that you are interested only in the highest ideals. Do all you can to live at peace with everyone.

The word of the Lord.

Shorter form

A reading from the letter of St Paul to the Romans 12:1-2. 9-13

Offering your living bodies as a holy sacrifice, truly pleasing to God.

Think of God's mercy, my brothers, and worship him, I beg you, in a way that is worthy of thinking beings, by offering your living bodies as a holy sacrifice, truly pleasing to God. Do not model yourselves on the behaviour of the world around you, but let your behaviour change, modelled by your new mind. This is the only way to discover the will of God and know what is good, what it is that God wants, what is the perfect thing to do.

Do not let your love be a pretence, but sincerely prefer good to evil. Love each other as much as brothers should, and have a profound respect for each other. Work for the Lord with untiring effort and with great earnestness of spirit. If you have hope, this will make you cheerful. Do not give up if trials come; and keep on praying. If any of the saints are in need you must share with them; and you should make hospitality your special care.

The word of the Lord.

✳ Reading 3

A reading from the letter of St Paul to the Romans 15:1-3. 5-7. 13

Accept each other as Christ accepts you.

Without thinking of ourselves, each of us should think of his neighbours and help them to become stronger Christians. Christ did not think of himself. And may God who helps us when we refuse to give up, help you all to be tolerant with each other, following the example of Christ Jesus, so that united in mind and voice you may give glory to the God and Father of our Lord Jesus Christ.

It can only be to God's glory, then for you to treat each other in the same friendly way as Christ treated you.

May the God of hope bring you such joy and peace in your faith that the power of the Holy Spirit will remove all bounds to hope.

The word of the Lord.

※ Reading 4

A reading from the first letter of St Paul to the Corinthians 6:13-15. 17-20

Your body is the temple of the Holy Spirit.

The body is not meant for fornication; it is for the Lord, and the Lord for the body. God, who raised the Lord from the dead, will by his power raise us up too.

You know, surely, that your bodies are members making up the body of Christ. But anyone who is joined to the Lord is one spirit with him.

Keep away from fornication. All the other sins are committed outside the body; but to fornicate is to sin against your own body. Your body, you know, is the temple of the Holy Spirit, who is in you since you received him from God. You are not your own property; you have been bought and paid for. That is why you should use your body for the glory of God.

The word of the Lord.

Reading 5

A reading from the first letter of St Paul to the Corinthians 12:31–13:8

If I am without love, it will do me no good whatever.

Be ambitious for the higher gifts. And I am going to show you a way that is better than any of them.

If I have all the eloquence of men or of angels, but speak without love, I am simply a gong booming or a cymbal clashing. If I have the gift of prophecy, understanding all the mysteries there are, and knowing everything, and if I have faith in all its fullness, to move mountains, but without love, then I am nothing at all. If I give away all that I possess, piece by piece, and if I even let them take my body to burn it, but am without love, it will do me no good whatever.

Love is always patient and kind; it is never jealous; love is never boastful or conceited; it is never rude or selfish; it does not take offence, and is not resentful. Love takes no pleasure in other people's sins but delights in the truth; it is always ready to excuse, to trust, to hope, and to endure whatever comes.

Love does not come to an end.

The word of the Lord.

✸ Reading 6

A reading from the letter of St Paul to the Ephesians 4:1-6

One Body, one Lord, one faith, one baptism.

I, the prisoner in the Lord, implore you to lead a life worthy of your vocation. Bear with one another charitably, in complete selflessness, gentleness and patience. Do all you can to preserve the unity of the Spirit by the peace that binds you together. There is one Body, one Spirit, just as you were called into one and the same hope when you were called. There is one Lord, one faith, one baptism, and one God who is Father of all, through all and within all.

The word of the Lord.

✖ Reading 7

A reading from the letter of St Paul to the Ephesians 5:2. 21-33

This mystery has many implications; but I am saying it applies to Christ and the Church.

Follow Christ by loving as he loved you, giving himself up in our place. Give way to one another in obedience to Christ. Wives should regard their husbands as they regard the Lord, since as Christ is head of the Church and saves the whole body, so is a husband the head of his wife; and as the Church submits to Christ, so should wives to their husbands, in everything. Husbands should love their wives just as Christ loved the Church and sacrificed himself for her to make her holy. He made her clean by washing her in water with a form of words, so that when he took her to himself she would be glorious, with no speck or wrinkle or anything like that, but holy and faultless. In the same way, husbands must love their wives as they love their own bodies; for a man to love his wife is for him to love himself. A man never hates his own body, but he feeds it and looks after it; and that is the way Christ treats the Church, because it is his body – and we are its living parts. For this reason, a man must leave his father and mother and be joined to his wife, and the two will become one body. This mystery has many implications; but I am saying it applies to Christ and the Church. To sum up; you too, each one of you, must love his wife as he loves himself; and let every wife respect her husband.

The word of the Lord.

Shorter form

⚜ A reading from the letter of St Paul to the Ephesians 5:2. 25-32

This mystery has many implications; but I am saying it applies to Christ and the Church.

Follow Christ by loving as he loved you, giving himself up in our place. Husbands should love their wives just as Christ loved the

Church and sacrificed himself for her to make her holy. He made her clean by washing her in water with a form of words, so that when he took her to himself she would be glorious, with no speck or wrinkle or anything like that, but holy and faultless. In the same way, husbands must love their wives as they love their own bodies; for a man to love his wife is for him to love himself. A man never hates his own body, but he feeds it and looks after it; and that is the way Christ treats the Church, because it is his body — and we are its living parts. For this reason, a man must leave his father and mother and be joined to his wife, and the two will become one body. This mystery has many implications; but I am saying it applies to Christ and the Church.

The word of the Lord.

✠ Reading 8

A reading from the letter of St Paul to the Philippians 4:4-9

Fill your minds with everything that is pure.

I want you to be happy, always happy in the Lord; I repeat, what I want is your happiness. Let your tolerance be evident to everyone: the Lord is very near. There is no need to worry; but if there is anything you need, pray for it, asking God for it with prayer and thanksgiving, and that peace of God, which is so much greater than we can understand, will guard your hearts and your thoughts, in Christ Jesus. Finally, brothers, fill your minds with everything that is true, everything that is noble, everything that is good and pure, everything that we love and honour, and everything that can be thought virtuous or worthy of praise. Keep doing all the things that you learnt from me and have been taught by me and have heard or seen that I do. Then the God of peace will be with you.

The word of the Lord.

✠ Reading 9

A reading from the letter of St Paul to the Colossians 3:12-17

Over all these, to keep them together and complete them, put on love.

You are God's chosen race, his saints; he loves you, and you should be clothed in sincere compassion, in kindness and humility, gentleness and patience. Bear with one another; forgive each other as soon as a quarrel begins. The Lord has forgiven you; now you must do the same. Over all these clothes, to keep them together and complete them, put on love. And may the peace of Christ reign in your hearts, because it is for this that you were called together as parts of one body. Always be thankful.

Let the message of Christ, in all its richness, find a home with you. Teach each other, and advise each other, in all wisdom. With gratitude in your hearts sing psalms and hymns and inspired songs to God and never say or do anything except in the name of the Lord Jesus, giving thanks to God the Father through him.

The word of the Lord.

✳ Reading 10

A reading from the letter to the Hebrews 13:1-4a. 5-6b

Marriage is to be honoured by all.

Continue to love each other like brothers, and remember always to welcome strangers, for by doing this, some people have entertained angels without knowing it. Keep in mind those who are in prison, as though you were in prison with them; and those who are being badly treated, since you too are in the body. Marriage must be honoured by all. Put avarice out of your lives and be content with whatever you have; God himself has said: I shall not fail you or desert you, and so we can say with confidence: With the Lord on my side, I fear nothing.

The word of the Lord.

※ Reading 11

✠A reading from the first letter of St Peter 3:1-9

You should all agree among yourselves and be sympathetic; love the brothers.

Wives should be obedient to their husbands. Then, if there are some husbands who have not yet obeyed the word, they may find themselves won over, without a word spoken, by the way their wives behave, when they see how faithful and conscientious they are. Do not dress up for show: doing up your hair, wearing gold bracelets or fine clothes; all this should be inside, in a person's heart, imperishable: the ornament of a sweet and gentle disposition – this is what is precious in the sight of God. That was how the holy women of the past dressed themselves attractively – they hoped in God and were tender and obedient to their husbands; like Sarah, who was obedient to Abraham, and called him her lord. You are now her children, as long as you live good lives and do not give way to fear or worry.

In the same way, husbands must always treat their wives with consideration in their life together, respecting a woman as one who, though she may be the weaker partner, is equally an heir to the life of grace. This will stop anything from coming in the way of your prayers.

Finally: you should all agree among yourselves and be sympathetic; love the brothers, have compassion and be self-effacing. Never pay back one wrong with another one; instead, pay back with blessing. That is what you are called to do, so that you inherit a blessing yourself.

The word of the Lord.

✠ ✖ Reading 12
A reading from the first letter of St John 3:18-24

Our love is to be something real and active.

My children,
our love is not to be just words or mere talk,
but something real and active;
only by this can we be certain
that we are children of the truth
and be able to quieten our conscience in his presence,
whatever accusations it may raise against us,
because God is greater than our conscience and he knows
everything.
My dear people,
if we cannot be condemned by our own conscience,
we need not be afraid in God's presence,
and whatever we ask him,
we shall receive,
because we keep his commandments
and live the kind of life that he wants.
His commandments are these:
that we believe in the name of his Son Jesus Christ
and that we love one another
as he told us to.
Whoever keeps his commandments
lives in God and God lives in him.
We know that he lives in us
by the Spirit that he has given us.

The word of the Lord.

❈ Reading 13

A reading from the first letter of St John 4:7-12

God is love.

My dear people,
let us love one another
since love comes from God
and everyone who loves is begotten by God and knows God.
Anyone who fails to love can never have known God,
because God is love.
God's love for us was revealed
when God sent into the world his only Son
so that we could have life through him;
this is the love I mean:
not our love for God,
but God's love for us when he sent his Son
to be the sacrifice that takes our sins away.
My dear people,
since God has loved us so much,
we too should love one another.
No one has ever seen God;
but as long as we love one another
God will live in us
and his love will be complete in us.

The word of the Lord.

Gospel Acclamation

Gospel Acclamation 1 Jn 4:8. 11

Alleluia, alleluia!
God is love;
let us love one another
as God has loved us.
Alleluia!

Gospel Acclamation 1 Jn 4:12

Alleluia, alleluia!
As long as we love one another
God will live in us,
and his love will be complete in us.
Alleluia!

Gospel Acclamation 1 Jn 4:16

Alleluia, alleluia!
Anyone who lives in love
lives in God,
and God lives in him.
Alleluia!

Gospel Acclamation 1 Jn 4:7

Alleluia, alleluia!
Everyone who loves
is begotten by God,
and knows God.
Alleluia!

Gospel Reading

✤ Gospel Reading 1

A reading from the holy Gospel according to Matthew 5:1-12

Rejoice and be glad, for your reward will be great in heaven.

Seeing the crowds, Jesus went up the hill. There he sat down and was joined by his disciples. Then he began to speak. This is what he taught them:

'How happy are the poor in spirit;
theirs is the kingdom of heaven.
Happy the gentle:
they shall have the earth for their heritage.
Happy those who mourn:
they shall be comforted.
Happy those who hunger and thirst for what is right:
they shall be satisfied.
Happy the merciful:
they shall have mercy shown them.
Happy the pure in heart:
they shall see God.
Happy the peacemakers:
they shall be called sons of God.
Happy those who are persecuted in the cause of right:
theirs is the kingdom of heaven.

'Happy are you when people abuse you and persecute you and speak all kinds of calumny against you on my account. Rejoice and be glad, for your reward will be great in heaven.'

The Gospel of the Lord.

✤ Gospel Reading 2

A reading from the holy Gospel according to Matthew 5:13-16

You are the light of the world.

Jesus said to his disciples: 'You are the salt of the earth. But if salt becomes tasteless, what can make it salty again? It is good for nothing, and can only be thrown out to be trampled underfoot by men.

'You are the light of the world. A city built on a hilltop cannot be hidden. No one lights a lamp to put it under a tub; they put it on the lamp-stand where it shines for everyone in the house. In the same way your light must shine in the sight of men, so that, seeing your good works, they may give the praise to your Father in heaven.'

The Gospel of the Lord.

✤ Gospel Reading 3

A reading from the holy Gospel according to Matthew 7:21. 24-29

He build his house on rock.

Jesus said to his disciples:
'It is not those who say to me, "Lord, Lord", who will enter the kingdom of heaven, but the person who does the will of my Father in heaven.
'Therefore, everyone who listens to these words of mine and acts on them will be like a sensible man who built his house on rock. Rain came down, floods rose, gales blew and hurled themselves against the house, and it did not fall: it was founded on rock. But everyone who listens to these words of mine and does not act on them will be like a stupid man who built his house on sand. Rain came down, floods rose, gales blew and struck his house, and it fell; and what a fall it had!'
Jesus had now finished what he wanted to say, and his teaching made a deep impression on the people because he taught them with authority, and not like their own scribes.

The Gospel of the Lord.

Shorter form

A reading from the holy Gospel according to Matthew 7:21. 24-25

He build his house on rock.

Jesus said to his disciples:
'It is not those who say to me, "Lord, Lord", who will enter the kingdom of heaven, but the person who does the will of my Father in heaven.
'Therefore, everyone who listens to these words of mine and acts on them will be like a sensible man who built his house on rock. Rain came down, floods rose, gales blew and hurled themselves against the house, and it did not fall: it was founded on rock.'

The Gospel of the Lord.

❦ Gospel Reading 4

A reading from the holy Gospel according to Matthew 19:3-6

What God has united, man must not divide.

Some Pharisees approached Jesus, and to test him they said, 'Is it against the Law for a man to divorce his wife on any pretext whatever?' He answered, 'Have you not read that the creator from the beginning made them male and female and that he said: This is why a man must leave father and mother, and cling to his wife, and the two become one body? They are no longer two, therefore, but one body. So then, what God has united, man must not divide.'

The Gospel of the Lord.

❦ Gospel Reading 5

A reading from the holy Gospel according to Matthew 22:35-40

This is the greatest and the first commandment. The second resembles it.

A lawyer, to disconcert Jesus, put a question, 'Master, which is the greatest commandment of the Law?' Jesus said, 'You must love the Lord your God with all your heart, with all your soul, and with all your mind. This is the greatest and the first commandment. The second resembles it: You must love your neighbour as yourself. On these two commandments hang the whole Law, and the Prophets also.'

The Gospel of the Lord.

✤ Gospel Reading 6
A reading from the holy Gospel according to Mark 10:6-9

They are no longer two, but one body.

Jesus said, 'From the beginning of creation God made them male and female. This is why a man must leave father and mother, and the two become one body. They are no longer two, therefore, but one body. So then, what God has united, man must not divide.'

The Gospel of the Lord.

✤ Gospel Reading 7
A reading from the holy Gospel according to John 2:1-11

This was the first of the signs given by Jesus – at Cana in Galilee.

There was a wedding at Cana in Galilee. The mother of Jesus was there, and Jesus and his disciples had also been invited. When they ran out of wine, since the wine provided for the wedding was all finished, the mother of Jesus said to him, 'They have no more wine.' Jesus said, 'Woman why turn to me? My hour has not come yet.' His mother said to the servants, 'Do whatever he tells you.' There were six stone water jars standing there, meant for the ablutions that are customary among the Jews: each could hold twenty or thirty gallons. Jesus said to the servants, 'Fill the jars with water,' and they filled them to the brim. 'Draw some out now,' he told them, 'and take it to the steward.' They did this; the steward tasted the water, and it had turned into wine. Having no idea where it came from – only the servants who had drawn the water knew – the steward called the bridegroom and said, 'People generally serve the best wine first, and keep the cheaper sort till the guests have had plenty to drink, but you have kept the best wine till now.'

This was the first of the signs given by Jesus: it was given at Cana in Galilee. He let his glory be seen, and his disciples believed in him.

The Gospel of the Lord.

✿ Gospel Reading 8
A reading from the holy Gospel according to John 15:9-12

Remain in my love.

Jesus said to his disciples:

'As the Father has loved me,
so I have loved you.
Remain in my love.
If you keep my commandments
you will remain in my love,
just as I have kept my Father's commandments
and remain in his love.
I have told you this
so that my own joy may be in you
and your joy be complete.
This is my commandment:
love one another,
as I loved you.'

The Gospel of the Lord.

✵ **Gospel Reading 9**

A reading from the holy Gospel according to John 16

What I command you is to love one another.

Jesus said to his disciples:

'This is my commandment:
love one another,
as I have loved you.
A man can have no greater love
than to lay down his life for his friends.
You are my friends,
if you do what I command you.
I shall not call you servants any more,
because a servant does not know
his master's business;
I call you friends,
because I have made known to you
everything I have learnt from my Father.
You did not choose me,
no, I chose you;
and I commissioned you
to go out and to bear fruit,
fruit that will last;
and then the Father will give you
anything you ask him in my name.'

The Gospel of the Lord.

❧ Gospel Reading 10

A reading from the holy Gospel according to John 17:20-26

May they be completely one.

Jesus raised his eyes to heaven and said:

'Holy Father,
I pray not only for these,
but for those also
who through their words will believe in me.
May they all be one.
Father, may they be one in us,
as you are in me and I am in you,
so that the world may believe it was you who sent me.
I have given them the glory you gave to me,
that they may be one as we are one.
With me in them and you in me,
may they be so completely one
that the world will realise that it was you who sent me
and that I have loved them as much as you loved me.
Father,
I want those you have given me
to be with me where I am,
so that they may always see the glory
you have given me
because you loved me
before the foundation of the world.
Father, Righteous One,
the world has not known you,
but I have known you,
and these have known
that you have sent me.
I have made your name known to them
and will continue to make it known,
so that the love with which you loved me may be in them,
and so that I may be in them.'

The Gospel of the Lord.

Shorter form

A reading from the holy Gospel according to John 17:20-23

May they be completely one.

Jesus raised his eyes to heaven and said:

'Holy Father,
I pray not only for these,
but for those also
who through their words will believe in me.
May they all be one.
Father, may they be one in us,
as you are in me and I am in you,
so that the world may believe it was you who sent me.
I have given them the glory you gave to me,
that they may be one as we are one.
With me in them and you in me,
may they be so completely one
that the world will realise that it was you who sent me
and that I have loved them as much as you loved me.'

The Gospel of the Lord.

Prayer of the Faithful

Taken from *Distinctive Weddings: Tying the Knot without the Rope Burns!* by Bláithín O'Reilly Murphy (Veritas, 2008) and *On the Way to the Wedding: The Complete Guide to Planning Your Wedding Ceremony* by Elizabeth Hughes (Veritas, 2006).

1. For N. and N., that their love for each other may continue to grow in the peace of Christ.

2. For N. and N. who now celebrate with us their joy and gratitude in receiving God's gift of love in the Holy Sacrament of Matrimony; that they may grow old together by sharing life's joys, struggles and challenges in order to become better persons and Christians. May the blessings of the Lord guide them through their lives as husband and wife.

3. For all married couples here today, that, witnessing N. and N. making their commitment of love, they renew their love for one another.

4. For the parents of N. and N., that they may be an example of love to their children.

5. For the parents of N. and N., who have given much of themselves to raise their children in the way God had intended, that he may bless them with good health and peace of mind.

6. For the family, relatives and friends of N. and N., who have been there to support them through the years. Bless them with God's love and peace always. We pray that God may grant them the happiness that they seek.

7. For all that are gathered here today to celebrate with N. and N., especially those who have travelled a great distance; that God will bless them and watch over them.

8. For all gathered for this celebration: may the joy of this day inspire our loving efforts and enrich the lives of our own family and friends.

9. For the deceased relatives and friends of N. and N., that God may shower them with eternal love.

10. For our loved ones who have gone ahead of us, that they may find eternal rest and happiness in the heavenly kingdom.

11. For the Holy Church and her leaders, Pope Benedict XVI, our Bishop N., and all our bishops, clergy and religious, that by their words and witness, they may continue to build God's kingdom of justice, peace and unity.

12. For the leaders of the Church: may the Pope and bishops so build up our Church that it will become the living sacrament of God's transforming presence in the world.

Reflections
and Blessings

(These should not be used in place of the scripture readings.)

'A Birthday'
by Christina Rossetti

My heart is like a singing bird
Whose nest is in a watered shoot;
My heart is like an apple-tree
Whose boughs are bent with thickset fruit;
My heart is like a rainbow shell
That paddles in a halcyon sea;
My heart is gladder than all these,
Because my love is come to me.

Raise me a dais of silk and down;
Hang it with vair and purple dyes;
Carve it in doves and pomegranates,
And peacocks with a hundred eyes;
Work it in gold and silver grapes,
In leaves and silver fleur-de-lys;
Because the birthday of my life
Is come, my love is come to me.

Sonnet 43
from Sonnets from the Portuguese *by Elizabeth Barrett Browning*

How do I love thee? Let me count the ways.
I love thee to the depth and breadth and height
My soul can reach, when feeling out of sight
For the ends of Being and ideal Grace.
I love thee to the level of everyday's
Most quiet need, by sun and candlelight.
I love thee purely, as they turn from Praise.
I love thee with the passion put to use
In my old griefs, and with my childhood's faith.
I love thee with a love I seemed to lose
With my lost Saints, – I love thee with the breath,
Smiles, tears, of all my life! – And, if God choose,
I shall but love thee better after death.

'Es Stephen Unbeweglich'
by Heinrich Heine

The stars, for many ages,
Have dwelt in heaven above;
They gaze at one another
Tormented by their love.

They speak the richest language,
The loveliest ever heard;
Yet none of all the linguists
Can understand a word.

I learnt it, though, in lessons
That nothing can erase;
The only text I needed
Was my beloved's face.

'My true love hath my heart, and I have his'
by Sir Philip Sydney

My true love hath my heart, and I have his,
By just exchange one for the other given.
I hold his dear, and mine he cannot miss,
There never was a better bargain driven.

His heart in me, keeps me and him in one,
My heart in him, his thoughts and senses guide;
He loves my heart, for once it was his own,
I cherish his because in me it bides.

'I love you for ...'
Anonymous

I love you
Not only for what you are,
But for what I am when I am with you.

I love you
Not only for what you have made of your self,
But for what you are making of me.

I love you
For the part of me that you bring out;
For passing over the many foolish and weak things
You find in me,
And for drawing out into the light
All the beautiful things only you could find in me.

You have done more for me than any creed.
You have made me feel my own goodness.
And all this you have done
With your touch,
With your words,
With yourself.
Thank you.

'On Marriage'
by Kahlil Gibran

You were born together, and together you shall be forevermore.
You shall be together when the white wings of death scatter your days.
Ay, you shall be together even in the silent memory of God.
But let there be spaces in your togetherness,
And let the winds of the heavens dance between you.

Love one another, but make not a bond of love:
Let it rather be a moving sea between the shores of your souls.
Fill each other's cup but drink not from one cup.
Give one another of your bread but eat not from the same loaf.
Sing and dance together and be joyous, but let each one of you be alone,
Even as the strings of a lute are alone though they quiver with the same music.

Give your hearts, but not into each other's keeping.
For only the hand of Life can contain your hearts.
And stand together yet not too near together:
For the pillars of the temple stand apart,
And the oak tree and the cypress grow not in each other's shadow.

Irish Marriage Blessing

May God be with you and bless you.
May you see your children's children.
May you be poor in misfortunes
And rich in blessings.
May you know nothing but happiness
From this day forward.

Traditional Irish Blessing

May the road rise up to meet you.
May the wind always be at your back.
May the sun shine warm upon your face,
And rains fall soft upon your fields.
And until we meet again,
May God hold you in the palm of his hand.

A Wedding Wish

Anonymous

All earthly goods I wish thee.
All that's good for thee and thine.
And still, not only earthly
But all we know to be divine.

May earth and heaven mingle
May earth and heaven be one.
All through your earthly journey
Till sets your earthly sun.

In sunshine and in shadow
Through dancing and in song,
May heaven bless your union
Throughout your whole life long.

A Blessing

Anonymous

May your home be filled with laughter and the warm embrace of a summer day.
May you find peacefulness and beauty, challenge, and satisfaction, humour and insight, healing and renewal, love and wisdom, as in a quiet heart.
May you always feel that what you have is enough.

A Marriage Prayer

Anonymous

Bless this marriage, as N. and N. begin their journey down the road of life together. May they respect each other's likes and dislikes, opinions and beliefs, hopes and dreams and fears, even though they may not always understand each other. May they rest in the knowledge that no matter what happens, by holding on to each other things will work out for the best. Most of all, dear God, help them to keep the torch of love burning with the fire that they now share in their hearts. Amen.

 ## The Way

Anonymous

The way is long – let us go together.
The way is difficult – let us help each other.
The way is joyful – let us share it.
The way is ours alone – let us go in love.
The way grows before us – let us begin.

Prayer of the Newly Married Couple

We thank you, Lord,
and we praise you
for bringing us
to this happy day.

You have given us to each other.
Now, together, we give ourselves to you.
We ask you Lord:
make us one in our love;
keep us one in your peace.

Protect our marriage.
Bless our home.
Make us gentle.
Keep us faithful.

And when life is over
unite us again
where parting is no more
in the kingdom of your love.

There we will praise you
in the happiness and peace
of our eternal home.
Amen.